T0195751

ALL SIMPLE THINGS BUT TIME

HOWARD BERNSTEIN

Order this book online at www.trafford.com
or email orders@trafford.com

Most Trafford titles are also available at major online book retailers.

Note: Some of Bernstein's poems printed here are from his
book *On Leave With Norgood*, San Diego Poets Press.

Printed in the United States of America.

ISBN: 978-1-4907-3355-5 (sc)
ISBN: 978-1-4907-3356-2 (e)

Library of Congress Control Number: 2014906823

Trafford rev. 02/11/2015

 www.trafford.com

North America & international
toll-free: 1 888 232 4444 (USA & Canada)
fax: 812 355 4082

This book is for Diane Dyas Bernstein.

Contents

Good Fortune

Good fortune, when I am dead,
may my poems be one time read
by a winsome summer's lass;
though she murmur, "Oh how crass!"
let her bestow her magic ring,
the glistening circle the iced glass brings
to the open page.

All Simple Things but Time

Time's perception is a puzzle.
Childhood's day seemed so very long,
awake at dawn, the early morn,
the summer's day
with swim and shower bath,
meals rushed through for endless play,
then dusk and the long sweet
end of day.
Time accelerates with age.
Morning toast and sweetened tea,
luncheon with the zenith sun,
and in half a wink,
"Can it be already five o'clock?"
and time for drink.
What makes our clock run slow then fast?
Is youth formed at the center of the Potter's wheel
and age spun outward towards the rim?
We know hub and rim
inseparably spin, yet each moves at
greatly different speeds.
Late summer flowers cut to the vase,
petal to the oaken floor,
the taste of snow will be upon the air.
All simple things but time
for childhood's sums of day plus day
were somehow multiplied away.

Between the Twitter and the Tweet

Our fingers can't stay still
between the twitter and the tweet.
The tinier the device,
the grander the paradox,
the broader the bandwidth,
the narrower is our life.
Our fingers can't "stand" still.
We're "Morphing Baby"!
Between the twitter and the tweet,
Our idols race by
swiftly, upon clay feet.

Treadmill, Life on the Run

Treadmill, life on the run
or, if you prefer, on the climb.
It is not the Classic shady stroll
where woodland nymphs and
nightingales hide in metered rhyme.
Now well lit,
the climb is upon a moving stair,
with the pinch of hurry.
It's a healthy bill of fare;
or try the treadmill's tread
programmed for hill and vale,
where earphones
sing to Nature
demurely dressed
in designer tights and sweats.
Life on the run, on the climb.
Is there a need
for Poets' shady brooks
when shapely Youth,
running,
demands
we take a look?

Tarry with the Check

Ah, the roast.
What cannot this genius chef do
even to the lowly toast?
Not to say, to Gâteau St. Honoré, or Profiterole.
Wait till you taste his crowning glory
Coup de cholesterol.
Forget not Lord Bacchus,
waves of reds and whites
burnish the pebbles on our way.
Lovers, friends, sisters, brothers. All
speak out in make-believe French, to gentle garçon,
comely waitress, guides to this day,
"l'addition, see vu play."
We shall bake the Piper in a cake.
We're brothers all,
what the heck.
Were not the cards of credit made
to tarry with the check?

One for Bacchus

Bacchus, dear Bacchus,
pardon, Dionysus, Olympic Greek,
for with the touch of age, one becomes more Roman
than classic Greek,
more like the wrinkled raisin than the perfect grape.
However, either God will do
when we seek escape.
Lecture, if you must, against the Juice!
Yes we know, of costly abuse.
Still for us Earthlings, liberating flights are sought,
though often our "High" hopes
will come to naught.

Then Feed Them Seeds of Age

Arthritic verbs and knuckle nouns
can't close around a simple verse.
Summer heat is air cooled
until we almost forget
what it is like to sweat.
My bird feeder is conquered by squirrels.
Damn their playful, fuzzy, frisky tails.
I'm preached to:
"They must also eat."
Then feed them seeds of age.

Winter chilblains follow, and
from my one good eye,
I spy the Goddess Athena and her nymphs.
My wool knit, out at the elbows,
once my Pride's possession, now is
just an old sweater.
Of such things,
the less said the better.

The Alumni Magazine

Column, dated numerals,
the newly minted class appears
and, with each succeeding issue, moves back
in the Mag, receding doors,
until it disappears.
There is always the dedicated Class Correspondent,
not lacking his or hers respondents:
Congrats, twin girls for the Whites . . .
Exec Jim Black fast tracks . . .
Joe Brown, as expected, "MD bound."
Years pass.
Nancy Legion wins *the* prize!
Makes our year proud;
I remember her as well endowed.
So it goes, John White, "early retire"
on a whim;
he will, he says, "teach
grandkids how to swim."
'37, '36, Class of Thirty-Five.
Are there really doorways to the disappear?
Can they still be alive?
John White, Jim Black, long gone.
Don't despair, or better yet, despair.
Joe Brown is going strong
and kept his hair.
Then,
where's our Class Correspondent and
his or her faithful respondents?
Maybe a nursing home, he or she,
still cannot let "passed" time be, but
with long-term memory, quite clear,
redreams the disappearing doors
of our Class Year.

Que Es La Vida?

What is life like?
Is it but the coarse joke:
"It's a baby's shirt, very short but not fragrant"?
Is it our constant travel confused with the journey?
The whiff of perfume, the sideway
glance, graceful motion?
Is it new thoughts or old?
The Harmony of sight and sound,
Ever changing but never changed?
Is it, is it
Winter dying
As tiny Snowdrops flower?

To Diane on Her Birthday

Daydreams of whimsy, yet profound
In sunshine's shadow, a golden crown, while the
Amaranth, flowers in your lovely eyes, as
New desire flickers but cannot die, for
Evening is but the herald of our new day.

On Leave with Norgood or Changing Planes at Cleveland

"Norgood," I said, "we borrow wonder as we fly."
Smoking, he half hummed, half spoke,
exhaling ancient poets with thinned-down smoke:

> Over men's heads, walking aloft,
> With tender feet, treading so soft.

In truth, above our heads there was but sky,
beneath our feet, puff clouds hid geometric fields
sown to winter wheat.
We landed at Cleveland to meet our dates.
They took us to church for All Souls' sake.
We tossed our spare change in the candle slot;
the girls knelt to pray.
O sweet impiety, the skimp of skirt, the lovely knee!
I glanced at Norgood,
but his thoughts were hidden in a hum.
God, I wonder where Norgood's got to?
I, for one, am back farming.

A pumpkin crop is in the fields;
dusk sets the pumpkin heads aglow.
A somber sight, like when they ranked and filed the troops
to test the man-made sun.
Silence shook the earth beneath our feet;
darkness mushroomed before the heat.
What was it that Norgood said?
"The bastard Hannibals never tell
the troops the Alps are cold.
Leaders gone mad, reducing humanness to dross,
denying the thread that must reweave the web
upon the common cross."
I must admit, I miss him some
since we changed planes at Cleveland.

N. G. Flake, Around the World

1. Airborne

"Reginald Phipps the Third, sir."
"N. G. Flake," I called my name.
"Stewardess, please,
drinks for Mr. Phipps the Third and me."
"Mr. Flake, my father, Phipps Two,
has given me London. How will it be?"
"Reginald, the lovely English girls
will treat you well."
So it went. Bar service ceased.
I passed my flask.
"N. G.," he slurred, "I'm glad I asked."
And back I smiled at young Phipps Three.

2. London

I bathed the travel weariness away and dressed,
went towards the Strand, turned west, cut through
the Embankment to walk to Charing Cross.
Bells tolled three.
I thought of Our Lord turning water into wine.
"O tidal Thames, I thirst."
The gibbous moon washed the sycamores
while poor men wrapped in newspaper sheets
slept beneath the lilacs in the park.
All great cities that I knew
had great rivers sweeping through.
Thoughts began to jumble in my head.
How long was it since Tinkle,
my travel clock,
woke me from my bed?

3. Munich, the Old Art Museum

Stone stairways rose, one east, one west.
I climbed east towards Eden.
There a painted garden grew, mysterious and deep.
There Eve, our pristine mother, stood.
My hand swept a serpent's trace in air
wanting to touch her beauty there,
knowing for a deed like this
the hero Oedipus paid with his eyes.
"Herr N. G. Flake." I turned.
"Herr Professor," I said,
"what a pleasant surprise!"

4. Zurich

She came through the airport gate.
I held a rose.
She wore Robin Hood's cap
silk stockings, tinted toes.
I touched her to see
if she were really there.
"Norgood, behave, you promised to be good!
I want a postal card
that shows a rich Swiss bank,
the hottest mustard and a frank,
the best, best Bordeaux wine,
I learned to drink
from you, you know."
She touched the rose.
"For God's sakc, Norgood, speak!"
For the first time that day, I spoke,
"At your command."

5. Hong Kong

"Shen Lee," I said, "beware of every word,
hang every creed by its painted toe,
inspect for knobby knees.
What care I if trees first grew on Chinese silk,
most times both East and West go wrong."
"Flake, nothing can be done with you."
"Agreed," I said.
She and her husband smiled.
We parted well as good friends part.
Day failed.
The ferryboats, like tiered castles,
sailed from violet skies.
Vanquished, their drawbridges fell.
The crowds surged, homeward bound.
I stood aside to watch the sea.
Night and singsong music touched.
The electric signs hummed,
"Wristwatch, wristwatch,
lose not a minute in a year."
I thought of my clock Tinkle
and the days we spilled.
Come, neon night!
No bells tolled.

6. Home

The elevator answered to my call,
floor by floor it rose.
She answered to the bell.
"Norgood, travel makes the man,
you're looking well."
I untied the seven dolls I bought,
set them round on seven chairs
and spoke "Bonjour" in seven tongues
to amuse our child.
Across a little bit of space,
I passed a velvet jewelry case that held
a beaten chain.
"Norgood, how very, very nice,
do you wish to try again?"

Norgood in His Dotage

Someone said, "He's gone old." It was
but the off day, for
juiced he gives his shirt away
and still seems filled
with springlike dreams,
though less driven.
Has love been spent?
His answer was hidden in his hum.
I think there may be some not lent
still waiting to be given.

Seventeenth of March

Puzzlements. The use of *lay* and *lie*.
Intransitive, transitive; objects taken or laid by.
A fine confusion, verbs and drinkers
regular and irregular
mixed in a bar before the parade starts.
German, Pole, Italian, we're all Irish,
proven by our pea ties and crepe clovers.
Flowers pinned on sateen vests
undulate with ladies' breaths
like shamrocks placed upon the emerald sea.
Through lace-trimmed glass
we see parochial school lads,
faces washed by youth;
they seem cocksure and unsure at the once.
A majorette in green beret
reminds someone of a girl we knew.
"Withdrew the world, she did, to pray."
Someone complains, someone consoles
as conversation ripples across the shoals.
The bugle bands are forming lines of march.
Rejoice! We are the present tense,
like sun through clouds.
Patrick, Patron Saint, is going with the crowds.

String Quartet in an Unheated Hall

It is bitter cold tonight, still
four gentlemen in thinnest evening tails
move as one.
Applaud appreciation and warm the hands.
What? A program change, Haydn for Mozart.
Why not? Did not old Franz Joseph weep
when young Amadeus died?
Come, sweet "Presto." Let
music bake the bread of paradise
while we dream of steaming soup.

A Poet Between Poems

Nurse,
down the polished hall, the pharmacy, the plastic glass,
flakes of crested, crystal ice, the splashing alcohol,
and one may cross Lethe's river stream.
Lie flat back and watch the sky.
Wild-beast clouds caress.
By miracle of mind and wind,
they thin to puffs of grapes
distilled upon the vine that
pour the sky
a glass of whitest wine.
What is more certain than summer come.
The midges humming dusk.
Uncounted Achilles, impatient of the wound.
The constellations turning on the sprocket of the night
among the fireflies in random flight.
The morning star upon the lip of dawn,
but you'll be gone about your rounds,
and I will relieve myself to an olden tree.

Have you never spoken to a tree?
O tree,
is it not beyond belief
that part of me that nurtured you
may come to leaf
beside the meadow's hedge
beneath a gibbous moon?
"Rest," she said, "rest."
The white starch shield before her breast.
Turning she read his chart.
"It tells the stirring of the winter's heart," he said.
The numbered diastoles, the numbered breaths,
filled almost to the full
like the growing moon above a wondrous realm,
the meadows' edge, the budding elm.

"Somehow It Will Come Right"

Ice cube poised between the teeth—and crunch
the desperate ritual of lunch—with Gin.
Stone the senses to a focused glare
then the mumbled, profane prayer
"Somehow it will come right."

The Edge of Farmlands

Steps, walkway, patch of grass,
the street,
a geometric plan, incomplete,
held in fields by poured concrete.
In spring, the fringes wet
with sprinklers, timer set;
in winter, tinged with snow.
On farmland's edge, row apartments grow.
The walls sieve sound.
At morning if you bathe,
you may hear the couple through the wall;
long hair blowing dry with guns ahum.
They are birds of sweet chirp, exotic coo.
"When I am rich," she calls to him . . . hum, hum,
"I give unto you."
"What?" he coos.
"Thirty-eight elephants trunk to tail, up the narrow stair."
They start to sing. Let them fly!
Like childhood's game of hide-and-seek.
The numbered doors in silence count,
"Ninety-eight, 99, 100 . . .
here we come, ready or not"
down the steps, walkway, past the patch of grass,
the street,
into down-paid cars
upon the poured concrete.
A geometric plan, incomplete,
upon the farmland's edge.

Walk through winter woods
to farmer's road,
November's pumpkins have been Halloween'd
from December fields
fallow and forlorn,
used up with stubble corn.
Upon a gaunt tree a crow
awaits the falling snow.
Along these back roads
in spring,
wildflowers will grow.
Their warm colors washed just short of bright
as though this chilblained day turning unto night
had somehow blanched the seed.
Even Aristophanes, the ancient Greek,
mocked this truth,
love of age for youth.
A sign upon the farmer's barn sells
"Grave Blankets and Christmas Wreaths."
The wreaths will come to mark
our numbered row of doors;
the blankets fringed with snow
will keep love warm.

The Devil at the Chessboard

Dare you approach the board serene
where prancing knights guard preening queens?
On with the game!

The Devil moves first by choice of white.
What fool thinks him prince of night?
A deceptive game.

For your defensive play you may try the French.
Victory's thirst for heady wine is rarely quenched.
The intoxicating game.

Midgame, midlife . . . forces in disarray.
Must the thoughtful player learn to pray?
A sobering game.

Do you detect the fiendish grin?
It's too late for the repentant win.
A desperate game.

Still the sinner may save his neck.
Hold the fuming Fiend in perpetual check.
Exciting but dangerous game.

For the Man Who Gave up Sleeping

When did it begin?
He did not know.
Was it evening with the filling of the drinking bars
that first he saw his sleepless self?
Was that his face reflected
from the mirrored whiskey shelf?
How pale he seemed among the
reddish golds of label stars.
Slowly as he went from sleep,
the kitchen chair became more than kitchen chair,
the long lathed legs pertly poised
beneath an undulating seat
while the backrest's gentle arcs and lines,
rising, bend upon the supple spines.
While all slept,
he read beside his potted plant.
Its leaves in greening preened
about the budlets barely seen.
Silence, deep silence
seemed to swell
before dawn murmurs distant bells.

He forced himself to concentrate upon the
book of battles that he read:
Wolfe Against Montcalm.
What powers did they not wield,
one dying of his wounds,
the other dead upon the field?
What designs are not woven with this thread,
woven midst the dying,
the living, and the dead?
He reclimbed the battlements
in the clearest darkness of his mind.
What could he see?
Beyond the fear of pain,
the rush of ecstasy,
beyond the Plains of Abraham,
the great river
running to the sea.

John Milton and the Ghost of Crazy Cohen

Where's the ghost of Crazy Cohen?
Has a high backhand lob, evening's arc of air,
carried him past the duckweed canals
past the stilled water ponds,
landing him in a dim-lit bar
beside his drinking pals?
Did he brush against their sleeve?
One friend said, "Crazy knew
there is no end to want. Didn't his hero
old Milton, the Puritan, reach for and
touch a young wife. Difficult life
knowing desire when your light is spent."
Like tossed stones that fall circles
in still water ponds, Crazy's words echoed
and were gone.
John Milton, Poet, impassioned and confined,
did you reach towards them from
the half-light of the blind
to caress the air
like the ghost of Crazy Cohen?

A Soldier's Leave

Seven days in London,
a chance to see the town.
On a cot at Charing Cross I lay,
a touch of flu, worst luck.
There were mugs of English tea
mixed with fevered dreams.
A sputtered bomb did fall, or
was it thrown shoes that jarred
the hostel walls?
I slept.
On the sixth night I wandered to Piccadilly
not for a woman but to stare;
I was weak and drunk on air.
Seven day-nights were gone.
Duffel bag in hand,
I stepped upon the moving train to Birmingham.
I think it's north? Strangely refreshed.
Did the sun break the sky?
I can't recall.

Winter Trip to the Keys

Across the ice, caked river smoke stacks rise.
Wind and smoke shape a feminine form.
Is it time to go?
Pack your case with a new floral shirt,
odd sheets of paper, spare lines, half-baked poems.
One scribbled sheet is on a "Final Notice!"
Are there special machines for
the dread of final notices?
They must be blueprint-built,
cast, milled, drilled, tapped, thread-bolted,
electrostatically sprayed, name-plated;
then they roll: Notice! Final Notice!
The smoke woman is still touched by the wind.
The journey starts by subway train.
The poster beauties have been gap-toothed
by marker pens. They smile at us.
Smell the kerosene of airport air.
Drink and crisp smiles will be served,
the cabin unbolted.
Heated air will dance before our eyes.
Shed your coat for the hibiscus shirt;
become a walking flower
under semitropic skies.
Evening and the drinking bars,
the grumble against all things done
and left undone.
The late-night hooting drunk
that splashes into tidal dawn.
Worthy of awakened scorn,
a tourist come, a tourist gone.

Little League Father, Class II

Superior was I to red-faced men,
fathers, caps banged against their legs,
yelling, "Safe I say!"
Until I watched "the lad," long-haired,
strong with intelligence
at Grand Tournament Chess.
Neither chastened by the rainy train ride
through poverty's backyard
nor taught simple grace by seeing
a blind man playing his board of squares,
I craved victory.
My boy to win!
Willed with greed
old as pawns.

Civil War Monument

Upon the cannonballs half-planted in the sunny park
children play a semicircle game of hop.
About them the North's honor roll
is carved on marble walls:
Sherman, Farragut, Grant,
Vicksburg, Harper's Ferry, Bull Run.
Now the fine-veined stones sadly bleed
spray-can scrawls:
"Avengers," "Sal 169."
Is it the desperate moment to be young
to want your leaders and your battle sung?

Civil War Monument, a Generation Later

Upon the cannonballs half-planted in the sunny park
children play a semicircle game of hop.
The marble walls scrubbed free of acrylic scrawls
still call the roll:
Sherman, Farragut, Grant.
But where are the Avengers and 169th Street's Sal?
Was it that desperate to have grown old,
to have the battles won and lost,
the story once more untold?

The 320 Bomb Group in Convention Convened

Resolved the 320 will masquerade tonight!
The airmen circle carpet corridors
descending floor by floor
dressed as dustmen, cowboys, villains, sheiks . . .
their women more subdued in classic evening gowns
with bodice silken bandage bound.
Even fabled Icarus is there
spreading cheesecloth wings.
Then amid the bursts of photobulbs,
certain as "Remember when,"
the Grand Ballroom will stand and sing.
Above the flashes of distant nights
their missions once were flown,
beneath those long-remembered flights
the seeds of terror sown.
One aircrew, now drunken, takes to the sky.
There's Icarus, first to play the fool.
From the high board his graceful bombing
dive hits the moon
pale shimmer on the hotel's pool.

Last Train from Newark

The poor must wait,
wait for the last train
steamed in rain,
delivered full-term
from stable sheds,
black Augean stable sheds.
Fearless Hercules
wets the rails in dread.
Transistors
wail and cry.
Carved umbrella heads, impaled,
dance with waiting legs.
Tan-skin woman
held rib-tight,
sweet baby held rib-tight.
Cloud-slashed, windswept
the spooked moon pales.
Pale horse, black rider
hear baby cry: 'Ride
ride, ride
that mother night
good-bye!'

Swann's Way

A generation has been born and blessed
since I laid your book to rest,
yet your fine-boned chain of themes
is fully fleshed within my dreams,
and memory gladly joins your quest
to flower buds at Odette's breast.

Desani Said

One bold thunderhead runs the seascape sky.
Over the sun
a moment's mock dusk
sets wings astir against the cottage screen.
They will have their bite
as all things will
and cling content above the windowsill
that holds the blanching shells,
cockle, Atlantic rib mussel, surf clam,
gathered by moonlight or flashlight
in the stealth of dark
or day's end pearl light.
Footprint and gull cry
almost saved, then lost to the surf.
No tern or laughing gull seen in brightest sun
no sand bug in its tidal backward dance,
for day would bring
the female form.
Hand upon knee, hand upon chest.
The oldest game:
"Pardon me,
did you know that Schubert was lonely"
or "Desani said, 'Love is pain on the installment plan.'"

Hand upon knee, hand upon breast,
wanting it to end and never end
both at once.
It is better to wait for night
and run. Run the rim of the sea
until the taste of blood is in your lungs.
Throw yourself upon the yielding sea.
Gaze upon the profaned moon
where men have dared to walk in dust.
Shaking, one drinks his whiskey neat,
eats sogged sandwiches trudging
towards a rented bungalow
and sleep.

Knees

It's enough to be alive,
to stroll the park like a cool breeze,
to boldly stare upon strange knees
and be chastened by
the loveliest of smiles.
It's enough to be alive,
to stroll the park
like a cool breeze.

"Bread," Said the President

"Bread," said the President, "it is good."
Has he fully understood
the banker's lien upon the land,
the farmer's note due on demand,
weather's need to watch the sky,
bending winds through wheat and rye,
the baker's diminished pride
the automated oven by his side,
the commuter's early slice of toast,
the "advanced society" of our boast,
our somewhat desperate game of "Drudge & Sums,"
lighthearted sparrow hops,
the toss of crumbs.

Pale Silks at Dusk

Our day is drawn closed on carbon chains.
Evening is undressed,
compressed against the curve of earth,
almost possessed.
The blighted elm, the thorn,
the scabrous sycamore
stand and wait with us,
each impatient of the night,
iridescent with loss of light.

The Twelfth House

Sunset let an artery for us while
we glisten with the leaf,
with the edge of threadbare park,
with the narrowing of twilight
spilling darkness into dark.
Are we but the educated clever
on the climb
informed of near and far
taking soundings of the shoals
steering course by neon star?
What is there that touched the heart?
Did we not march for Sharpeville,
but were we bruised by others' wounds?
All things we do
are done in fits and starts.
This summer it is the Zodiac.
She reads aloud,
"The Twelfth House
is of the hidden enemy, our own undoing."
"Yes," he said, "that house of dread
that rises with us from our bed
and shaves in our looking glass."
He laughs, she laughs, we laugh.
Are we only of the present tense
weary of the climb?
No one guessed, we temporized
and mostly missed the mark
as sundown bled darkness into dark.

Mingled and Beguiled

Have you dreamed the dream in which
the living touch the dead,
quickened as one they were, mingled and beguiled,
each touched by each with the amaranth of smile?
We watched the sea as evening came,
wondering if dreams are thread from
childhood's cloth unwound?
Perhaps it would be the other way around,
and from the dreaming past, new
meaning could be found?
At day, we awoke still dreaming, mingled and beguiled,
awoke to coughs from other rented rooms,
to whatever web we spin,
to the ephemeral once more waiting to begin.

Grandfather

In summer's intensive heat,
they dressed me in my sailor suit to meet
an old man gone deaf.
He took his dead son's son by the hand.
For many, many years,
I felt the chill of those childish fears.
Now that I have also come to winter woods,
how gladly would I once more meet that olden man.
How simple it would be to understand.

One for Joyce,
Announced with Child

Music pulsed,
syncopated,
her breath, half-bated,
sang
jukebox songs,
half-sung, half-prayed,
mostly believed.
Sweet, puzzled love
conceived.
Turn towards her lovely face,
sweet Mary,
Mother of Grace.

For Sigmund Semmel (1956-1980)

And simpler yet,
they will past perfect us,
as shadows brushed beneath a lovely eye,
washed, brushed, and then blown dry,
a moment's slenderness, caressed.
Give us drink
for his spider plant has fallen shoots;
kiss their greening parachutes,
kiss them with a dioxide kiss.
Fill his chipped enamel cup
from the chipped enamel sink.
How were we to know
he would be watered but by rain?
Which dream of his will we not dream again,
which of ours was lost with him?
He slept, waked, and sleeps
beneath the high-iced clouds,
evening's ribs of mackerel sky
the promise of the fair,
a saddened kiss fallen on the air,
a slender moment lost.

The Wake

The handshake and the hug,
the "How are you and yours,"
the job that every Monday hates,
the scrimped for, hoped for, dreamed of
midst the cull of common fate?
Console the grieving wife
still so full of life, buxomly thin.
One cannot say
it may be days
perhaps while getting drunken
or looking to the sea
that one will first miss the friend.
Yes, we know, one by one
they'll dress us in our Sunday's best
when also called to take our rest.
Still most mourners entering
kneel and pray.
Has not the inexorable always been invoked?
Between a handshake and a hug
we move towards the smoking room to smoke.

On Leaving Rented Rooms

When we have left these rooms and gone
and the new couple have come,
will some part of us remain,
something from our task workdays,
the stipends and complaints, the weekend wished
and gone with weekend speed?
We leave the sun upon the windowsill,
the memory of music, the now and then,
exquisite thrill.
What else from our life,
now packed into a borrowed van,
will remain?
Of course, when the new couple come,
they could not care,
for of despair they'll bring their own
and probably just reconnect the phone.

Winter Dream Before Sleep

Dream before sleep,
I lay not shriven,
south by southwest
towards the sun
driven.
Paper-cup wine,
the imagined roast
served on beds of buttered toast
are soon devoured
in my darkened garden,
wallpaper-flowered.
Double bolts bar the door
while iced night is glaced
like a petit four.
I lay not shriven,
south by southwest
towards the sun driven.

Poetry Reading at a Women's College

This is a College Girl town in winter.
Deep snow, frozen bright, holds
clapboard houses. White on white.
The bland dorm walls feed the compulsion
to decorate, create, paste, project;
some reverberate with Schubert punches,
others with Rock and Roll.
"Tell us about your poems." What can one say?
My girl loves her dog? Grandfather grows old?
Two young women give a smoking gift,
excusing generosity as "a bad roll."
With the loveliest of smiles, they go the dance,
sailing on liquid hips, perhaps, to Lesbos Isle.
Door panels have been meticulously painted
pinks and blues;
handmade Valentines are hung.
We are obsessed to create, decorate,
to come above ourselves.
If we could reach, we'd repaint stars.

Postcard from London

If we were but together,
we would wild-dream, prevaricate,
pray to Sin.
I would fill the Savoy's marble tub,
listen for your splashes within.
Would you unlock the door?
Would you let me talk of Christian Art,
pretending those Catholic magic spells
were not written in your blood?
Would we catch night fever
throwing dice again and again,
breaking fast on sausages and gin?
Having drunk too much,
would I make you curse and cry?
Would we become weary, saddened,
delirious with pain?
Touch, swear, "Never again."
I am alone;
my life runs out of hand.
I write a postcard,
"Greetings from a distant land."

Stolen Stones

Tell polite lies so we may meet,
and let the Gideon Bible preach:
"Woe unto you, woe unto you."
Gentle chambermaid dusting dresser tops,
will you let the open bible sing
the Song of Solomon,
"love without woe"?
The answer is, "Probably no."
All is drink and clear as crystal spheres.
All held within reach
within a rented room.
The scholar's game of lost and found:
great cities sifted mound by mound,
captive women scattered to the fecund valley fields,
scattered beneath seasons' suns.
Once great marble scrolls, broken and unrolled,
are used for cutting stones.
Parchment poems are burned for cooking heat.
The trodden fields, sown, resown.
Our profane curses, our sweet songs, reborn.
Seed unto grain, grain unto seed.
"Do you sleep, do you sleep?"
"No."
"Come rest," she said, "come rest."
Eyes like the morning star,
love like stolen stones.

Earth and Air

We were of different signs,
Earth and Air.
Turning to go her way,
inertia held her by the hair,
then losing grip as she spinning spun,
flung a golden helmet like a gift of sun.
She walked away.
I watched her faded blue jeans fade
and from long-failed, stumbled French,
spoke the universal everywhere,
"Mon Dieu, quelle derriere!"
We were both lost and found,
nine parts impure, one part profound.
We rode her old red car, walked the beach.
She had natural grace
and let a freckle touch her face.
She believed that we are guided by our stars.
I laughed as once I laughed when told
that tilted on our poles,
we sail ellipses about a third-rate star.
How many windless reaches through the sky
had I, while she but twinkled in her Daddy's eye?
We were of different signs, Earth and Air.
How could she understand, someone who could not love?
How does one explain
spring's lovely hand in winter's glove?

Bus Tour from Salzburg
to Burchtesgarden

From the old city where Mozart was born,
pass baroque churches, tourist stands, sounding horns,
and go along the river's way.
Late summer scenes are bus window-framed.
Grazing cows and ripening grain are held in still-life air
and here and there
the roadside shrine
the cross
high above wild flower beds,
crown of sorrows, brow that bled.
The climb towards the Eagle's Nest begun.
Is this not where the Madman danced
about and wildly spoke,
taking pleasure as the ovens smoked?
Had not Mozart in some unmarked grave slept,
might he not have wept?
"Berchtesgarden, one hour pause," the tour guide spoke.
The Italian lady smiled; she would take a wine,
the American a coke.

Madrigals

Madrigals are
angelic octave climbs,
free falls of pure voice tones,
halftones, glides,
the thread of melody
spun about the medieval world,
bannerettes of unicorns unfurled.
Alchemy's air to precious golden curl.

Journey

Steaming coffees are sipped
with cautious kisslike sips as
varicolored tickets wave good-bye,
rainbowed against
the vaulted station sky.
The train is drawn on polished
silver rails as city's land
bound concrete bands
slowly expand to valley lakes.
Distant mountains wear rain-brimmed clouds.
One moves through many cars to dine.
The braided waiters
weaving side to side
seem to sway the train.
Straight vineyard-tended rows
suddenly scatter to and fro.
Change vision's arc and you
change the vision and the vines.
Beyond meadows, darkening depths of storm.
On the speeding train raindrops rest
upon the windowpane,
then touch and run on.

Beethoven

When first I heard *Fidelio*,
woven with a wondrous weave of song,
I knew life is well made.
Surely, Beethoven must have his dying wish
to hear again in Heaven.
For how could the angels aflutter
forego
celestial harmonies
that echo from the dust of plains below?

They Fall Easy That Have the Spare Couch for Bed

Once they gave us darkness with a dollar clock,
and silence
was distilled with each ticking tock.
Now there's clever clocks
with digit eyes.
What have those damn spies of night to spy?
The birth of dawn upon a foldout bed,
another day and spread
upon the make-believe of "Grandma's Bread."
Yes, the wrapper clearly says,
"Good to Eat"
(bleached from finest artificial wheat).
"Thank you, thank you, for we must go."
Fold the moth-laced blanket that warmed the tired toe.
Some say we are leaves before the wind.
But are we not
the melody's continuo,
the chorus in rented gowns
that transcends the song.

O

Need one more foolscap sheet be filled
when "Silence is the most perfectest herald of joy"?
Is that line quoted correctly? Can't tell
for my soft-backed references, pages nicotined by time,
my compendiums, encyclopedia, even *Shakespeare Complete*
and my dog-eared King James are boxed
in a borrowed basement
wrapped safely with the Genius Wizard Chess Set,
which one could beat
once you learned patience
and let the batteries wear down.

Still I have a dictionary and a sea view.
Fair trade?
Mostly, except when the sand is too tan
the water too blue, the sky too sky with
sailboats ballooning red-white, blue-white stripes
and one suddenly tires of looking on "that scene,"
mother to countless motel room lithos.
Happily the sea's side cannot stay still
and the sand goes gray-white as dusk,
color-blinds those banal spinnakers.
Then ring-billed gulls flock and roost
motionless and silent,
staring into the wind at whatever mystifies them.

Digressing. I must come back to quoted "Lines."
Good Fortune's child is early read to.
Whether it be Nursery Rhymes or A. A. Milne,
early verse lines indelibly persist
only to be lost like Genius Wizard Chess
when the batteries finally run down.

Memorized school poems?
If your teacher called upon you across the years,
would you not still raise hand ready to recite?
Some even try courting with borrowed lines.
My favorites were Siegfried Sassoon's:

> A moment's passion closing on the cry
> O beauty born of lovely things that die!

What fair heart worthy of the prize could resist?
A few.

Then someone said, "Why not?"
Why not cut the foolscap to blank pristine strips
of white—write and paste upon the old front door.
Day by day one-liners found their gum-taped way.

> The glory that was Greece
> The grandeur that was Rome

Quotes from Gilgamesh, the Testaments, Shakespeare,
Poets East and West.
Finally there was barely space to fit one's key,
and one could ponder there to dinner called.

Then someone else said, "Why not?"
Why not distill. Take them off one by one
until but one remained.
Like the pimple in paradise it could not be ignored.
"Invictus" was the first to go.
Then more than one genius lost his place
in each day's dilemma.
Finally two slips remained.
William Cowper's haunting lines:

>   Each in his own delusions; they are lost
>   In chase of fancied happiness, still wooed
>   And never won . . .

And Sassoon's:
>   O beauty born of lovely things that die!

Then . . . I had always known Sassoon would win.
Everyone knows the elements,
tempests, inclemencies, infidelities,
time its very self—
books stored, bag packed, I took one last
look back at the great chipped enamel door,
so scarred with tape skeletons
even the winner had been diminished;
all that remained was our symbol, the letter
O

Will She Gaze and Wonder Why?

Swept and bound around by wind and bending trees,
she walks beneath the Southern Cross,
breathing sweet breaths breathed,
nicotined into the night.
Her cigarette ash,
the dart of fireflies,
a fallen star are also sparks in summer's sky.
Will she gaze and wonder why?
A cut rose waits upon a water glass;
the wine is chilled.
Will she tire and come to rest
veiled in purest shine, as though
the moon had bathed a star in sparkled wine?

Procrustes

Procrustes, robber, brute,
none sing of you.
A long gold earring danced about your head,
terror striker,
that cut or stretched
to fit the iron bed.
Still who will not know thievery,
another's thoughts or deeds,
purloined renown?
Do not stolen gems sparkle
on the stolen crown?
It is said your last wanton glance was bold,
coveting dawn's first ray of gold
even as Theseus cried,
"Knave!"
across the gleam of swords.

Saint Patrick's Cathedral

A candle is lit with prayer,
the lost wax flows
as cathedral stained glass hues
arterial, venous reds and blues
deepen with late afternoon.
Tourists with their guidebooks out
mingle with the faithful and devout;
salt-and-peppers, brunettes, reds,
a sprinkle of golden heads.
Many sign the cross, synchronized somehow
with their short and shallow altar bows.
The organ's solemn tones
echo against the ancient stones
announcing Mass.
The priests adjust their vestment stoles;
each plays a role,
salt-and-peppers, brunettes, reds,
the sprinkle of golden heads,
celebrants that pass.

Poets at Winter's Party

Inhaling smoke into their minds,
they watched space distort through casement blinds.
Below, the icy road wound through the park.
Beyond, a river ran to sea.
Above, a sliver moon.
Slowly dusk gave up its ghosts to dark,
as car lights turning on
seemed but odds and ends of spark.
"The crescent moon holds evening's star,"
one poet said. The other smiling replied,
"Yes, there flies Near East's bannerette in western skies."
The hostess said, "Come dine."
It was simple fare, casserole, bread, wine.
Someone's girl, radiant and somewhat high,
began reciting lines:

> Hand me my coupon book of schemes
> Payments due for this night's dreams.

The poets smiled for words were winter's party,
their abiding, unrequited love.
Did it matter that one
had taken hot baths that day,
the other needed winter gloves?

Suburbia

Given half the chance,
will we not tinker to enhance
what once was semiwilderness?
Across the well-kept lawn,
the silent goslings trail
the plastic mother goose
into a silent dawn.
The bush, the vine,
countless hybrid varietals flower
and are doing fine
as are most native trees
except our blighted elm,
sadly overwhelmed.
Who is not to say
our somewhat commercial smoky way
has not helped a cloud?
Summer's day, why not, when air is still
a man-made stratus cloud may come to rest
upon a man-made hill.

On Seeing My Picture
Taken Unaware

I would keep my image in my mind,
a gracefully aging gentleman
welcome as baking bread.
Why shoot me unaware,
shortsighted to a book of poems,
sprouting ears, sparse graying hair?
Where is that once wondrous curly crown?
Gone with the flood of years
that left the gullies of a frown.
Many, past the first blush,
would keep their picture in their mind.
Why see time?
Why pour silver salts upon the wound?

In Memory of Bernie

Maybe somewhere, you'll wait for me,
perhaps Kowloon by China's sea? The throng,
the very crush of crowds, the loneliness of dusk,
may let us meet.
Smash punches to the arm
with boastful, youthful strength
cry splendor with a rage that breaks
the binds of weekly wage.
We would taste the charcoal-spiced air,
drink the neon bars.
We would ask the dark-haired lovelies to dance,
to dance until the neons dimmed,
until the possible was gone
and one is left whistling
in a distant, windless dawn.

One for the Moon

It snowed last night.
Plowed, the streets are plainly bright,
the sky is clearly cliché blue.
A daylight sliver moon, ghostly white,
will become a silver slice tonight.
Each of our moons is bought with time.
With their waxing, waning shine, we spend.
New moon, embossed
credit card without the thought to cost
arise!
Our streets are freshly plowed,
the snow piled high. Spend your
saved-up silver for the gift
of winter sky.

Sweet Memory

In stilled night sometimes I see
a long-ago familiar face
but lose the name.
Sweet memory, speak to me,
be equal to such a simple task
for now there is
no one left to ask.

Perhaps It Is a Leaf

Is time unseen
and invisible expanding sphere
turning on the Greenwich Mean
precisely through the year;
or is it a more palpable belief
to think, perhaps it is a leaf?
The leaf that pulses spring.
The leaf that tells the summer's breeze.
The leaf that blazes fall,
whose nodal bud awaits
beneath the winter's snow.
It goes
either way.
Good morrow to your morn.
Good evening to your day.